This Book Belongs To:

....

....

....

....

....

....

....

....

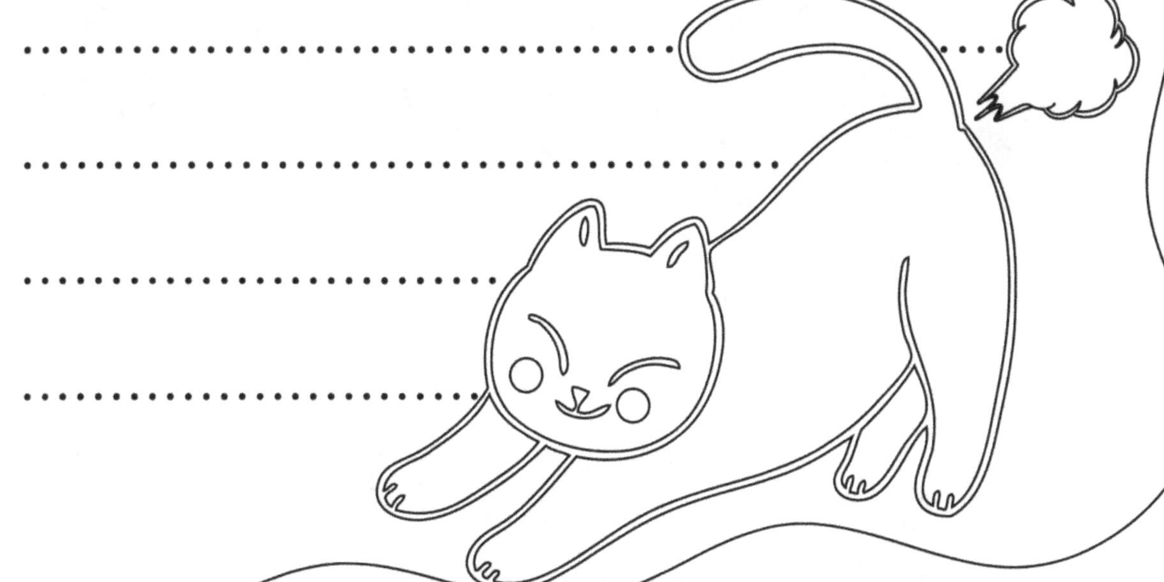

ISBN: 9798672919959

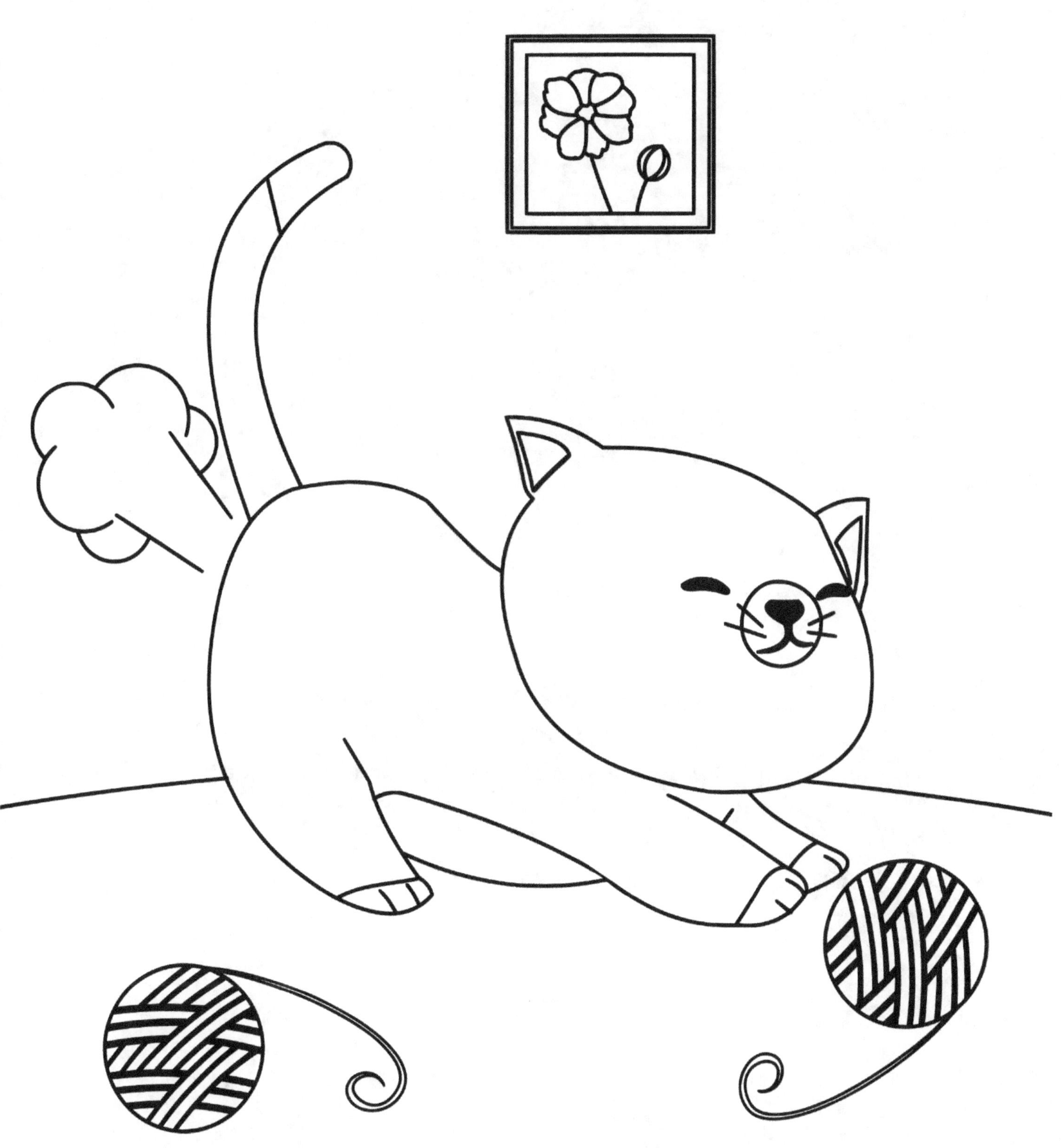

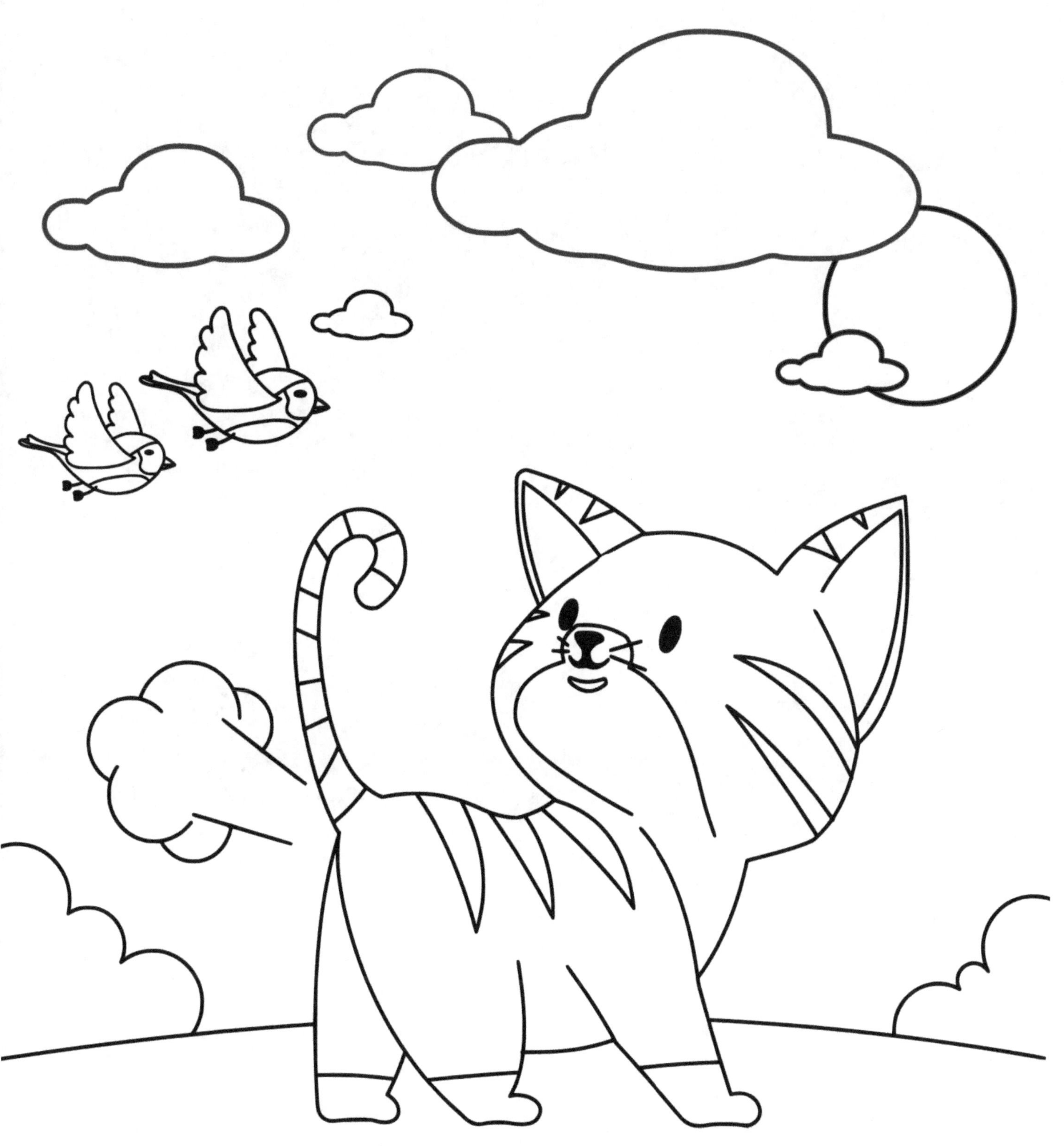

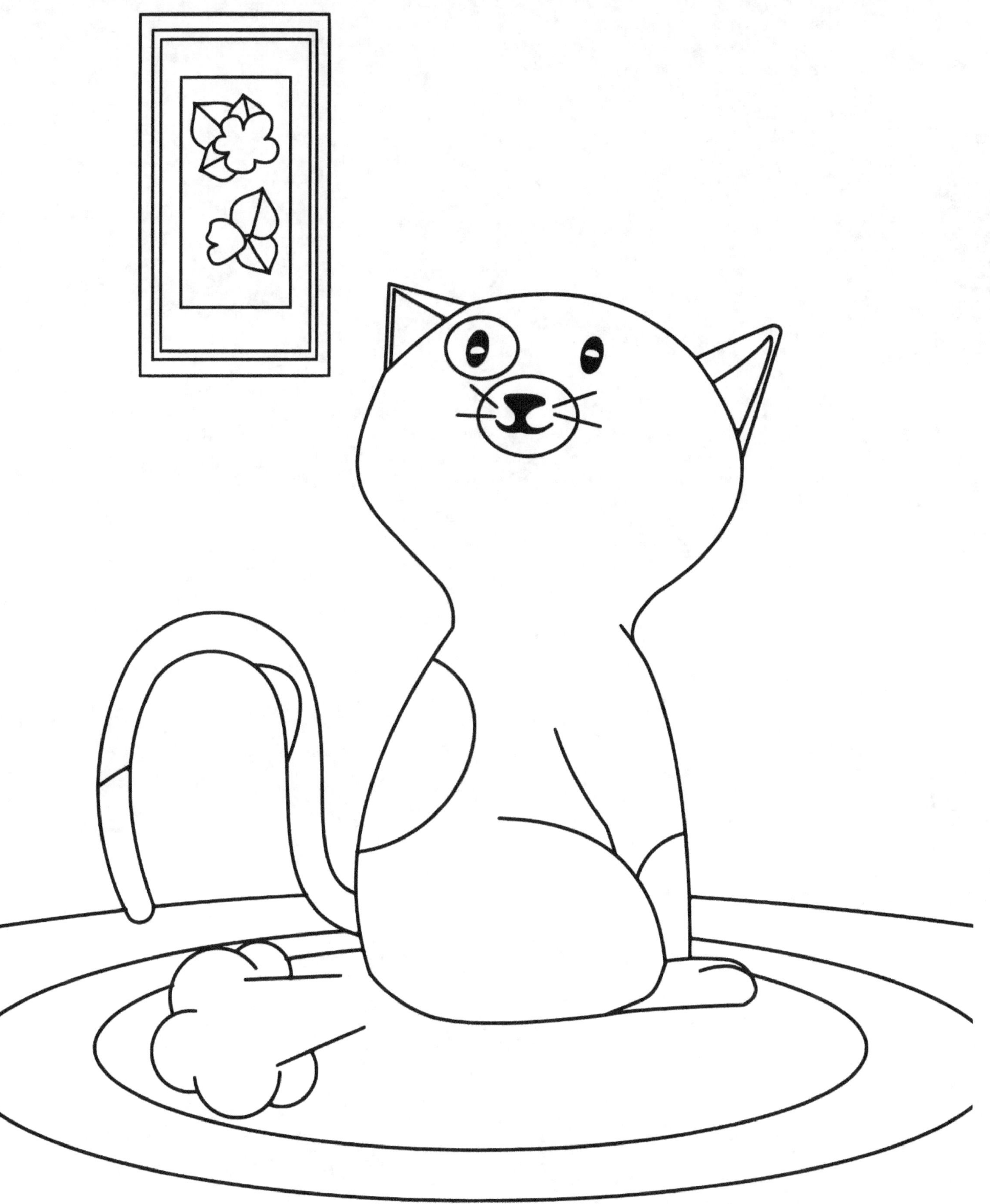

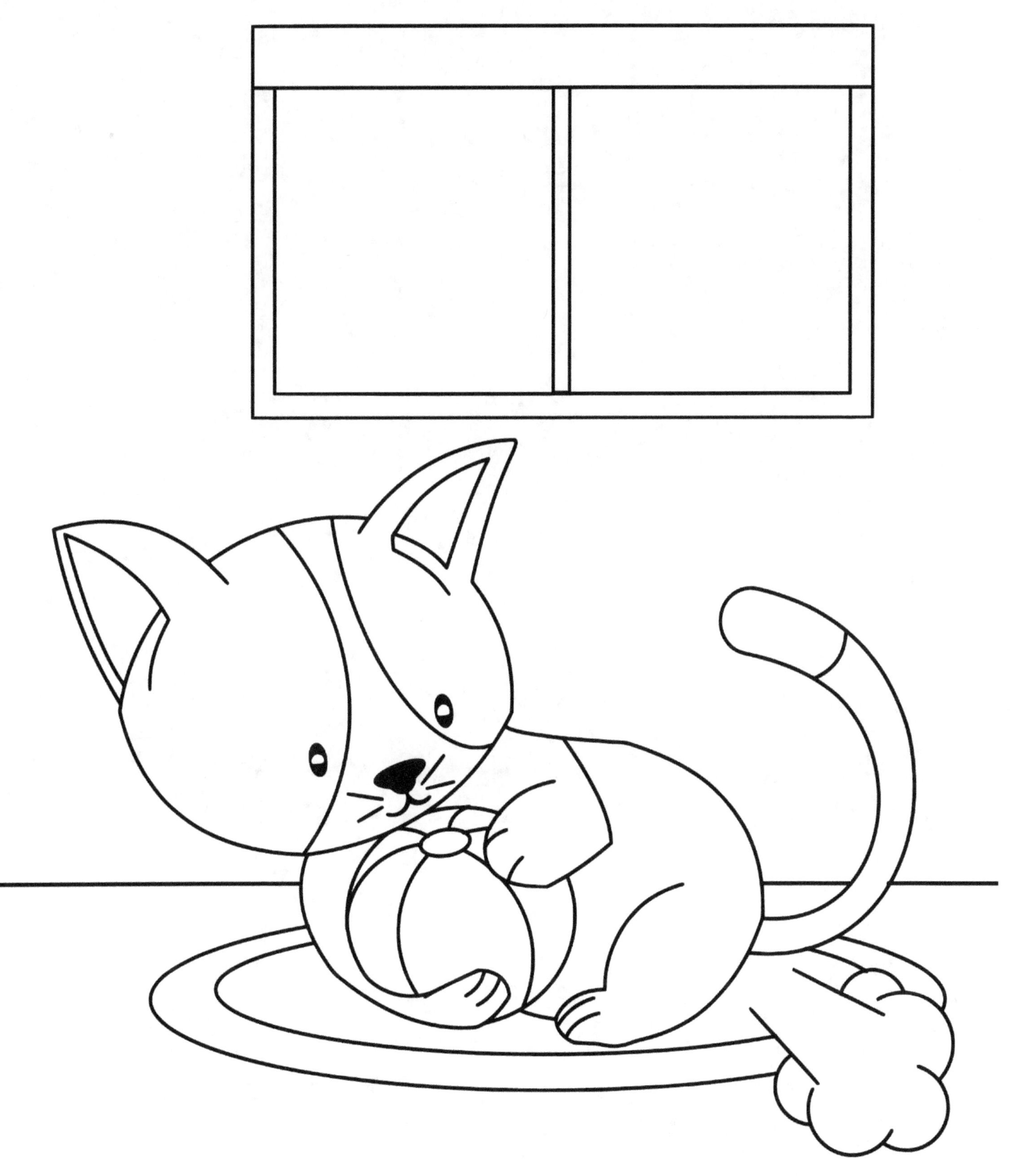

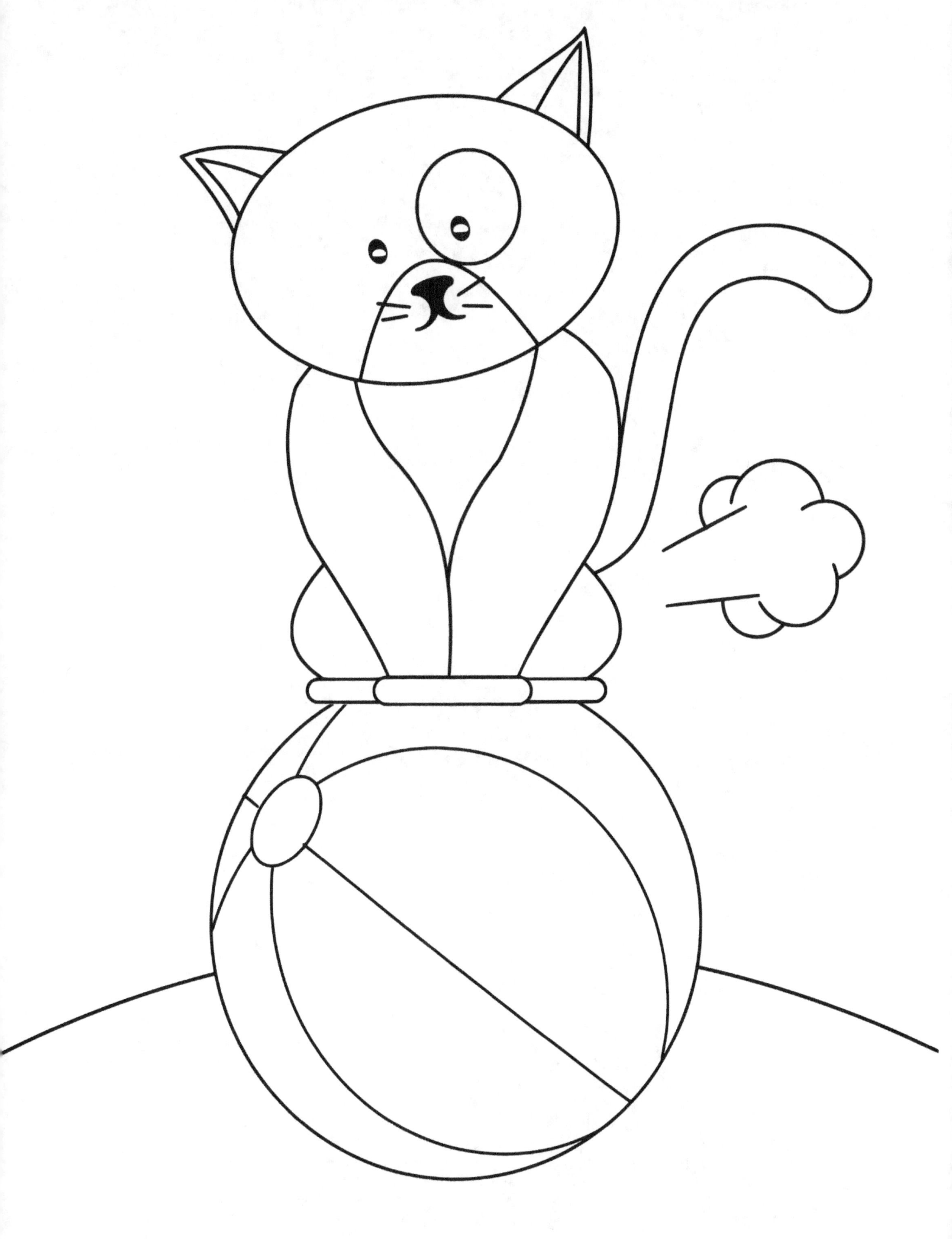

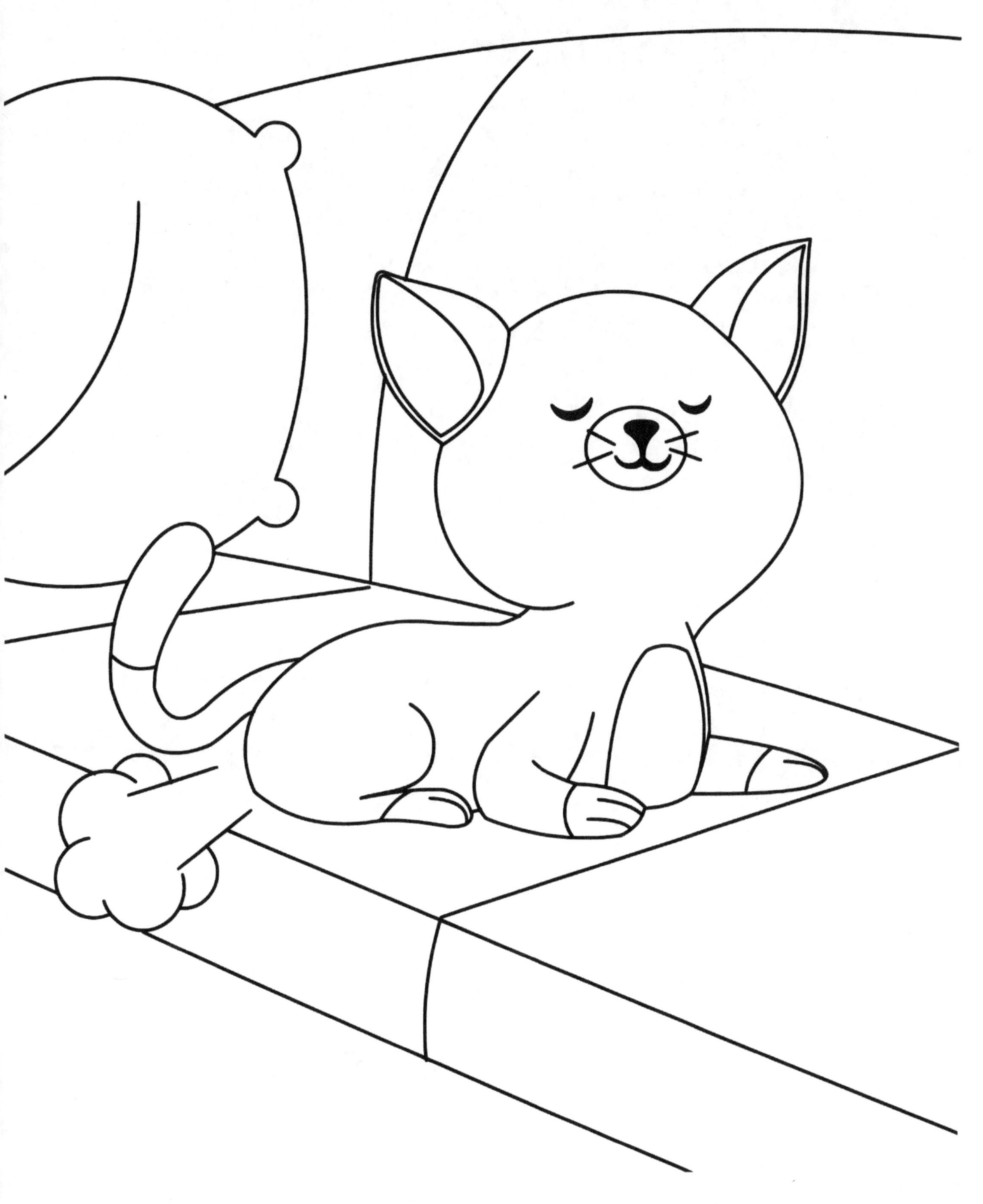

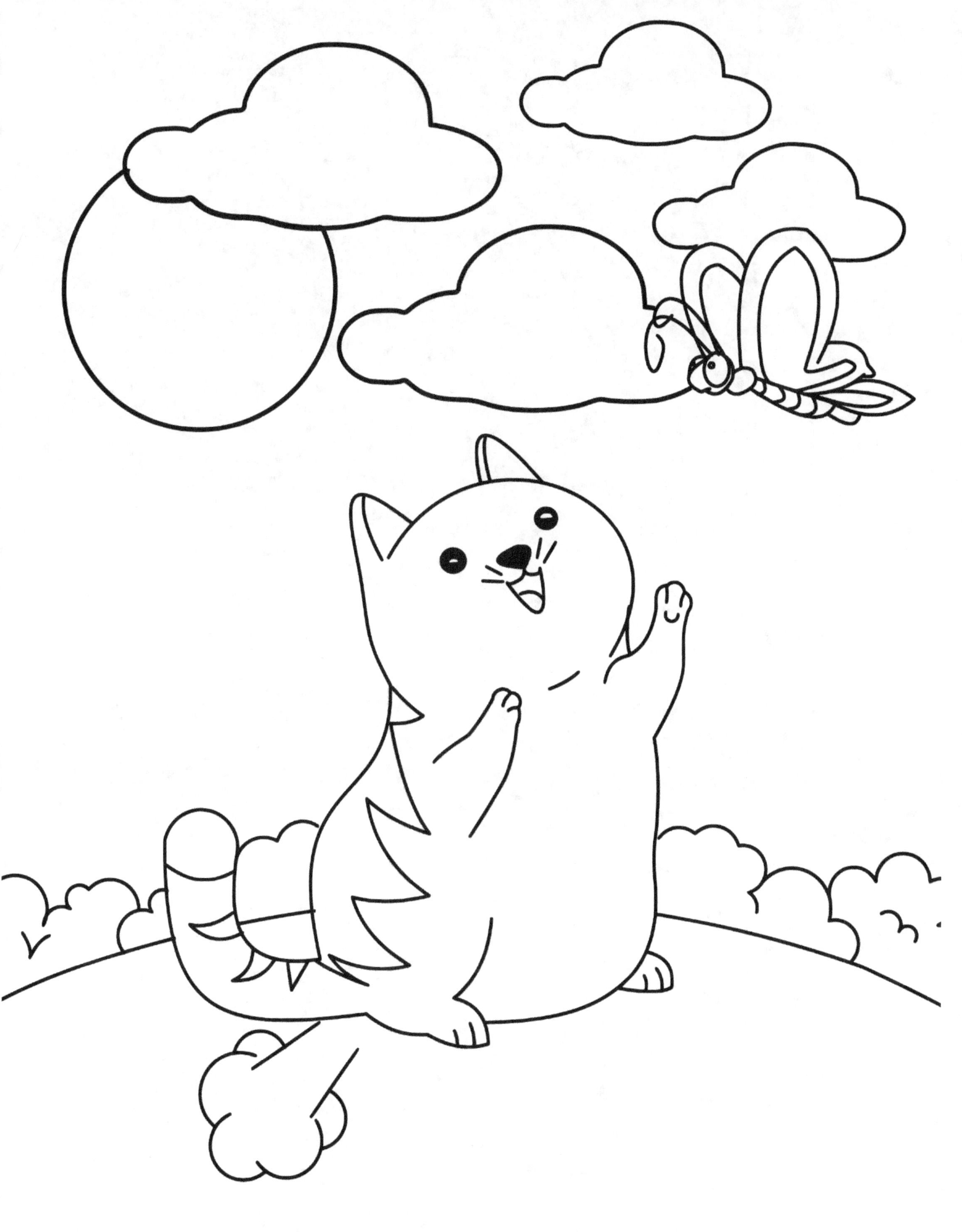

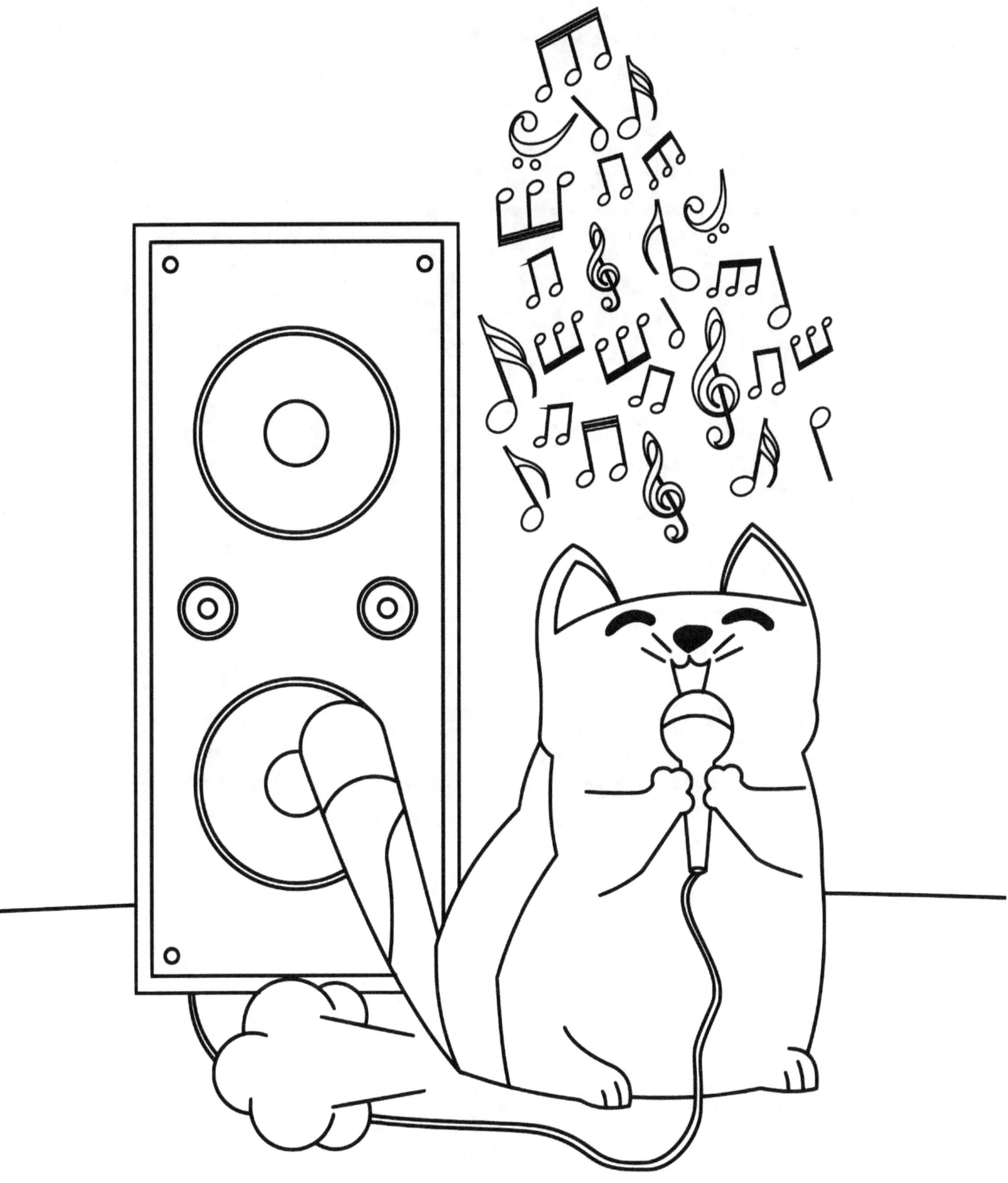

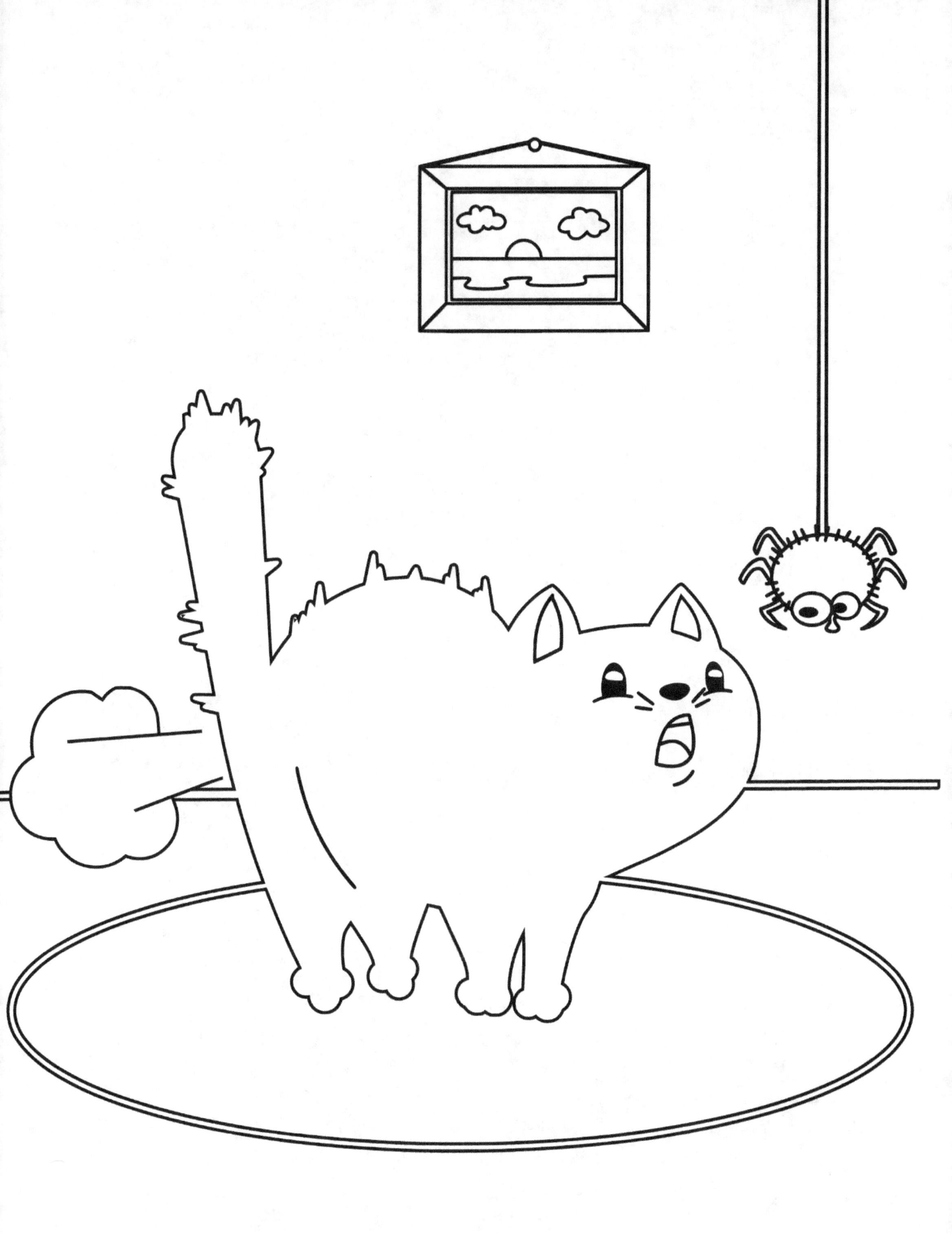

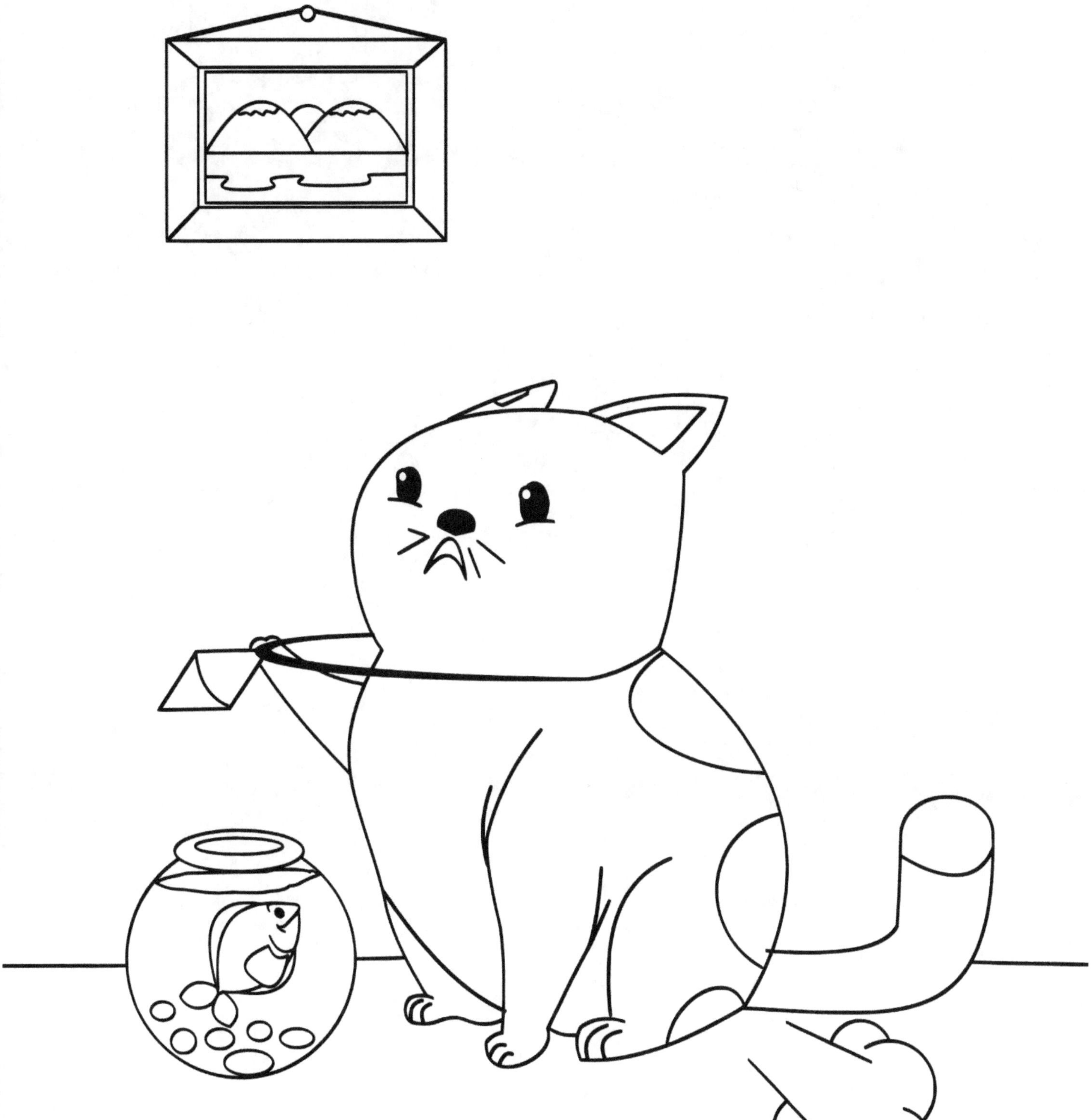

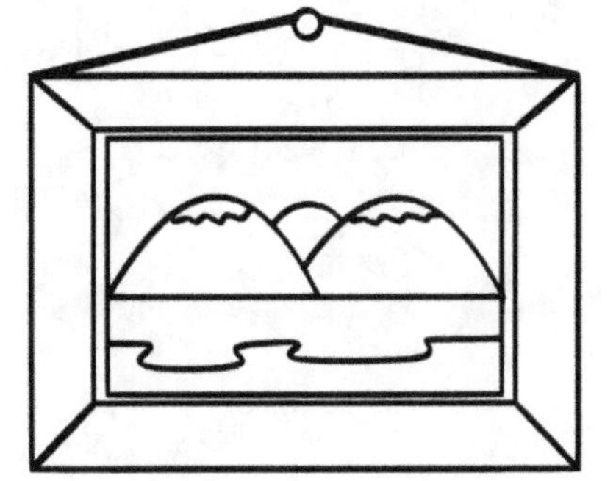

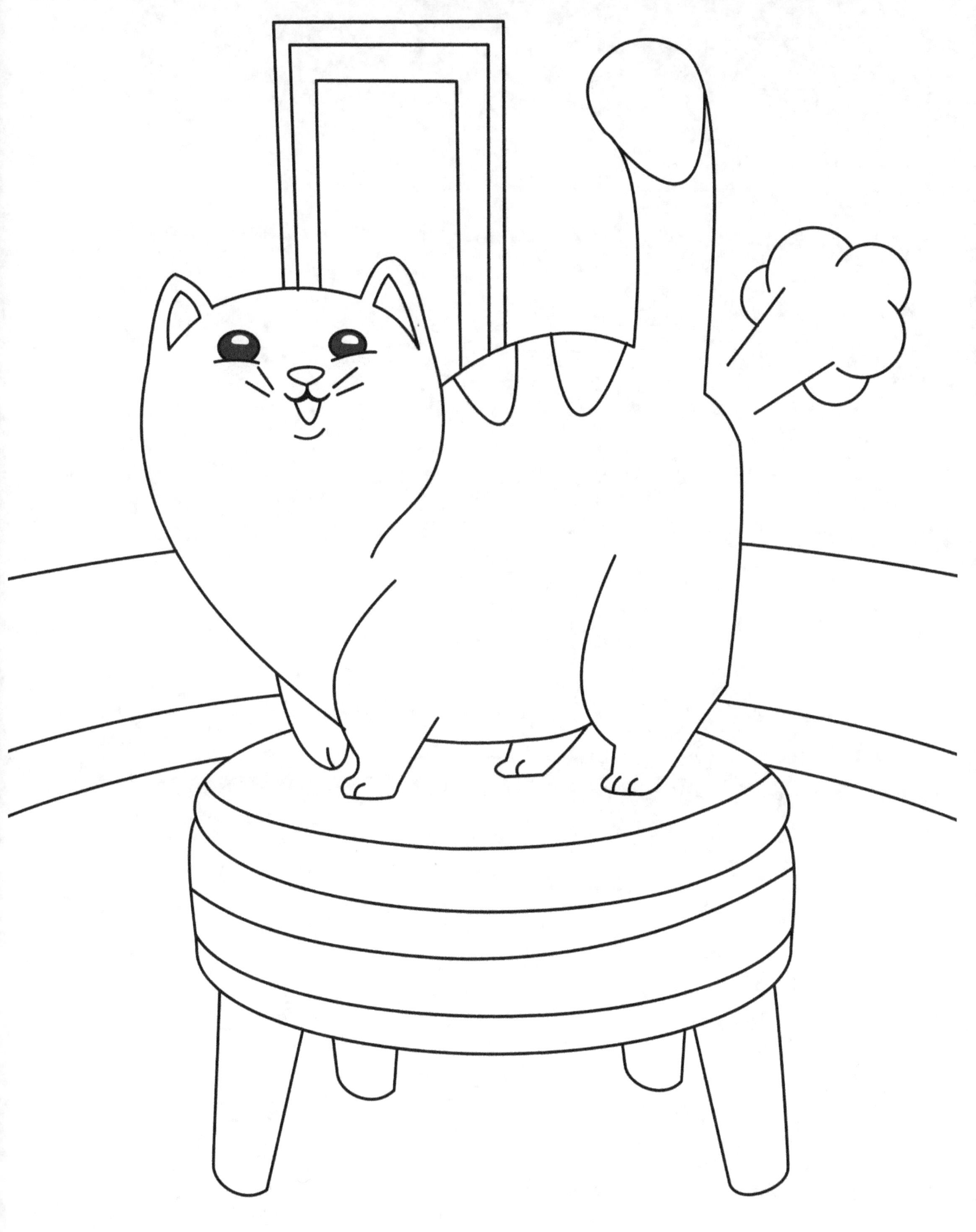

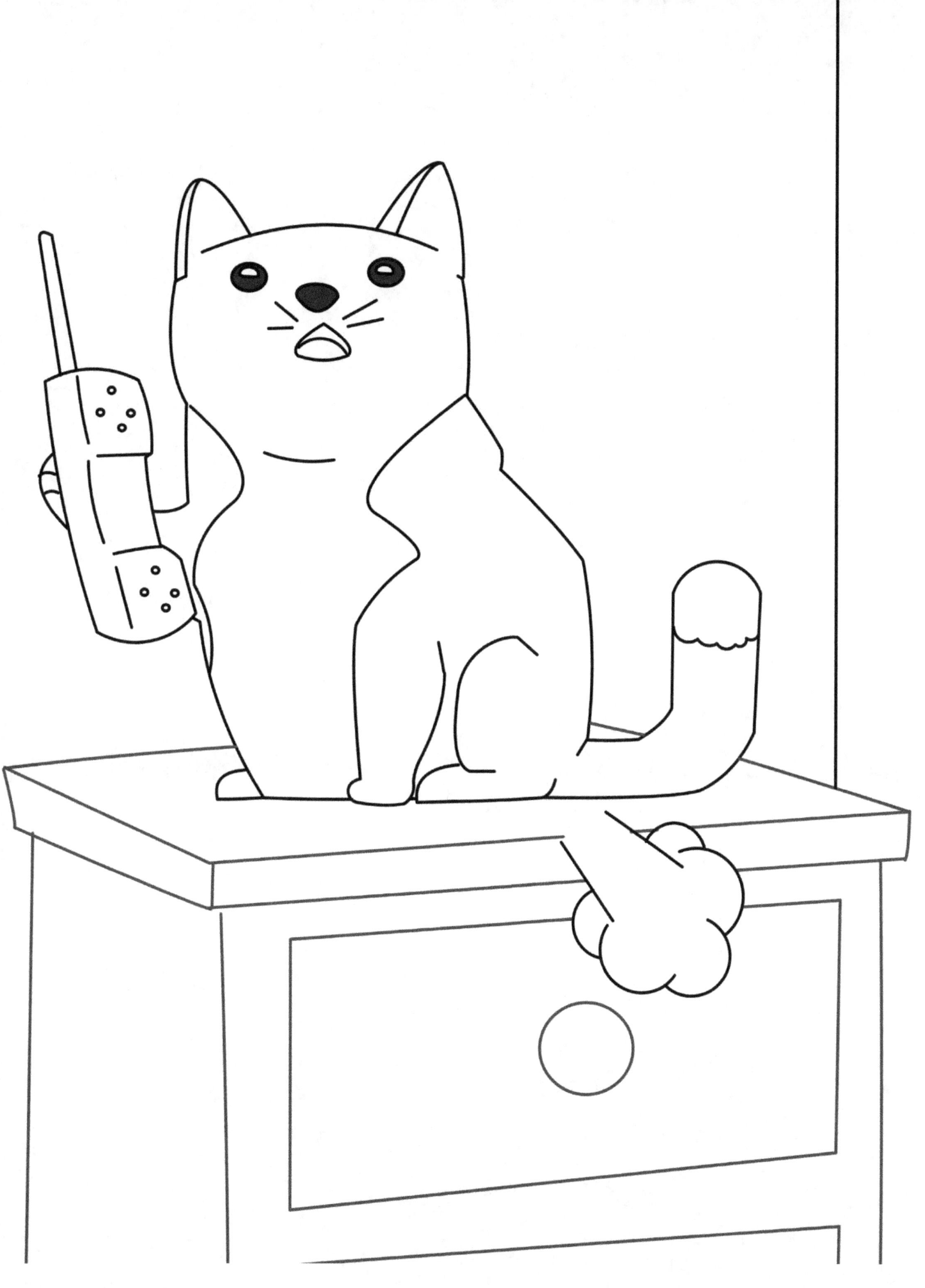

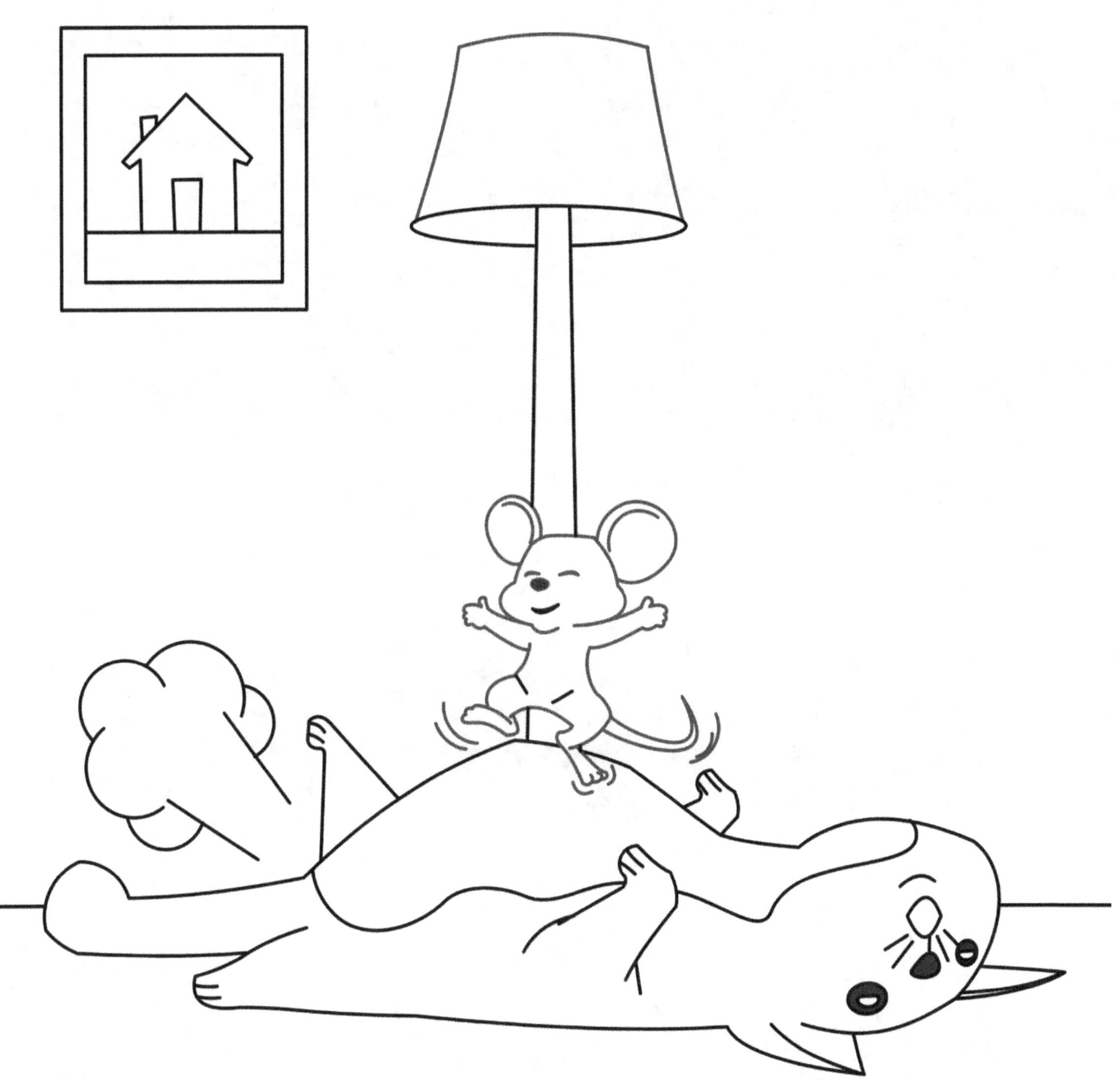

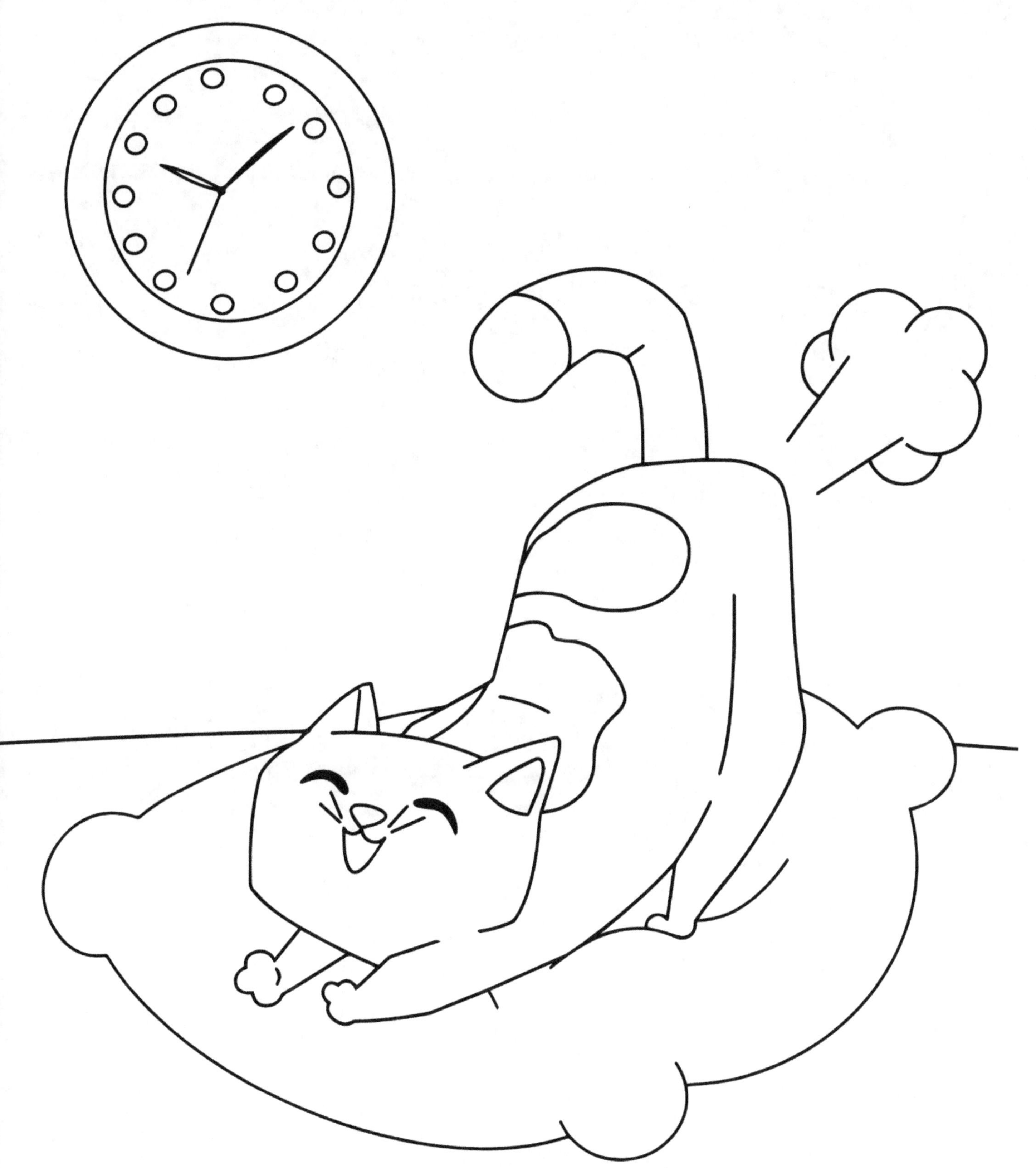

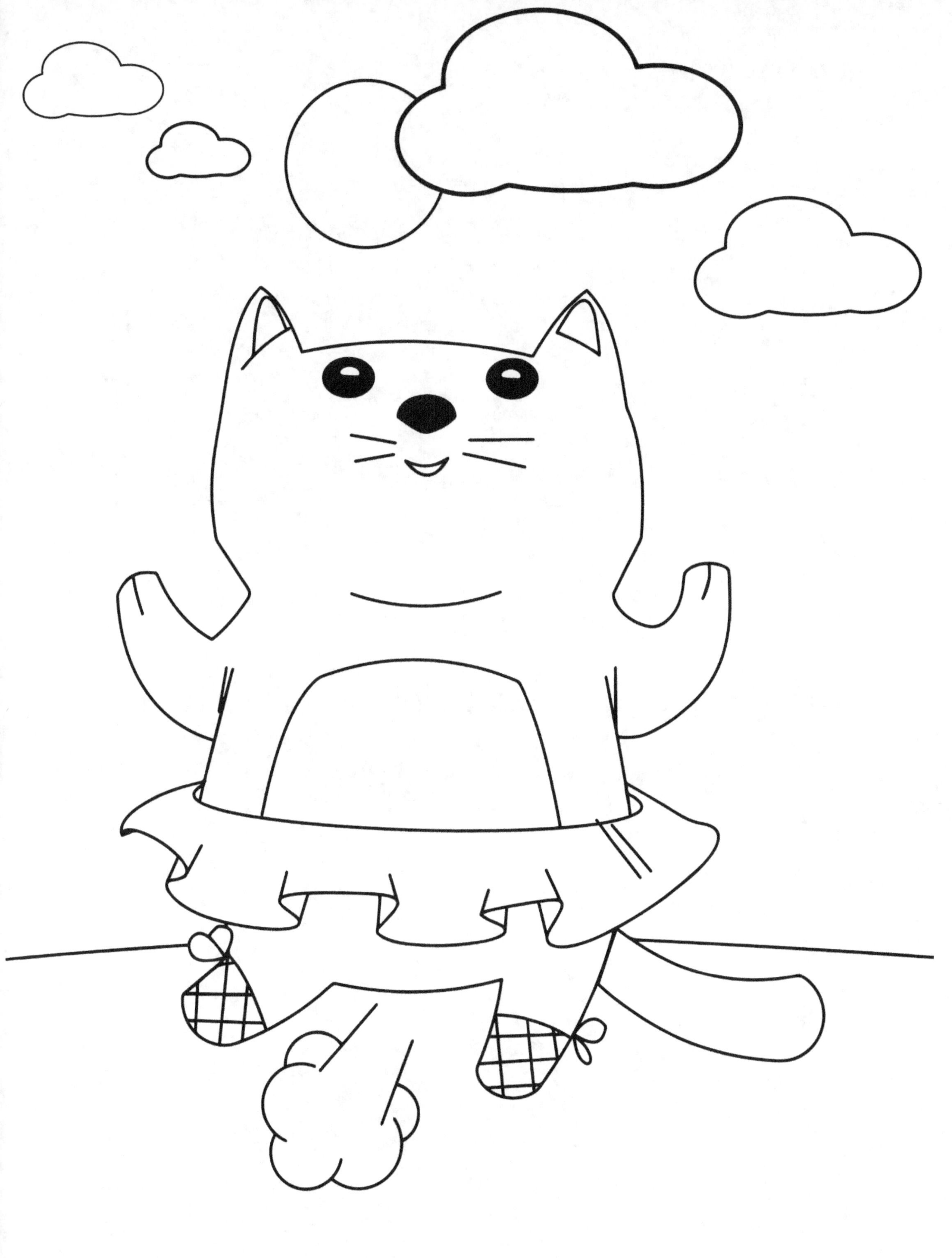

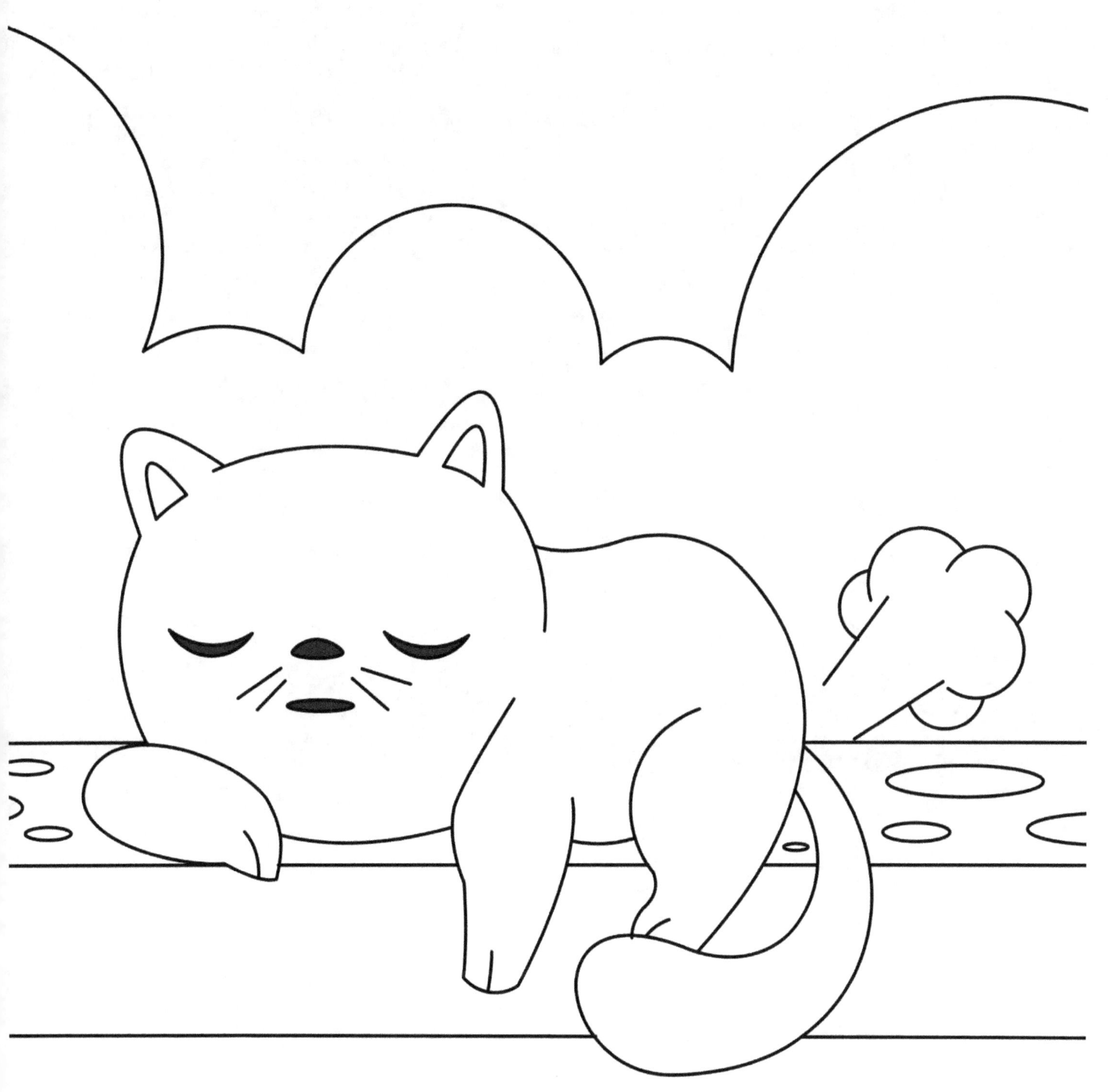

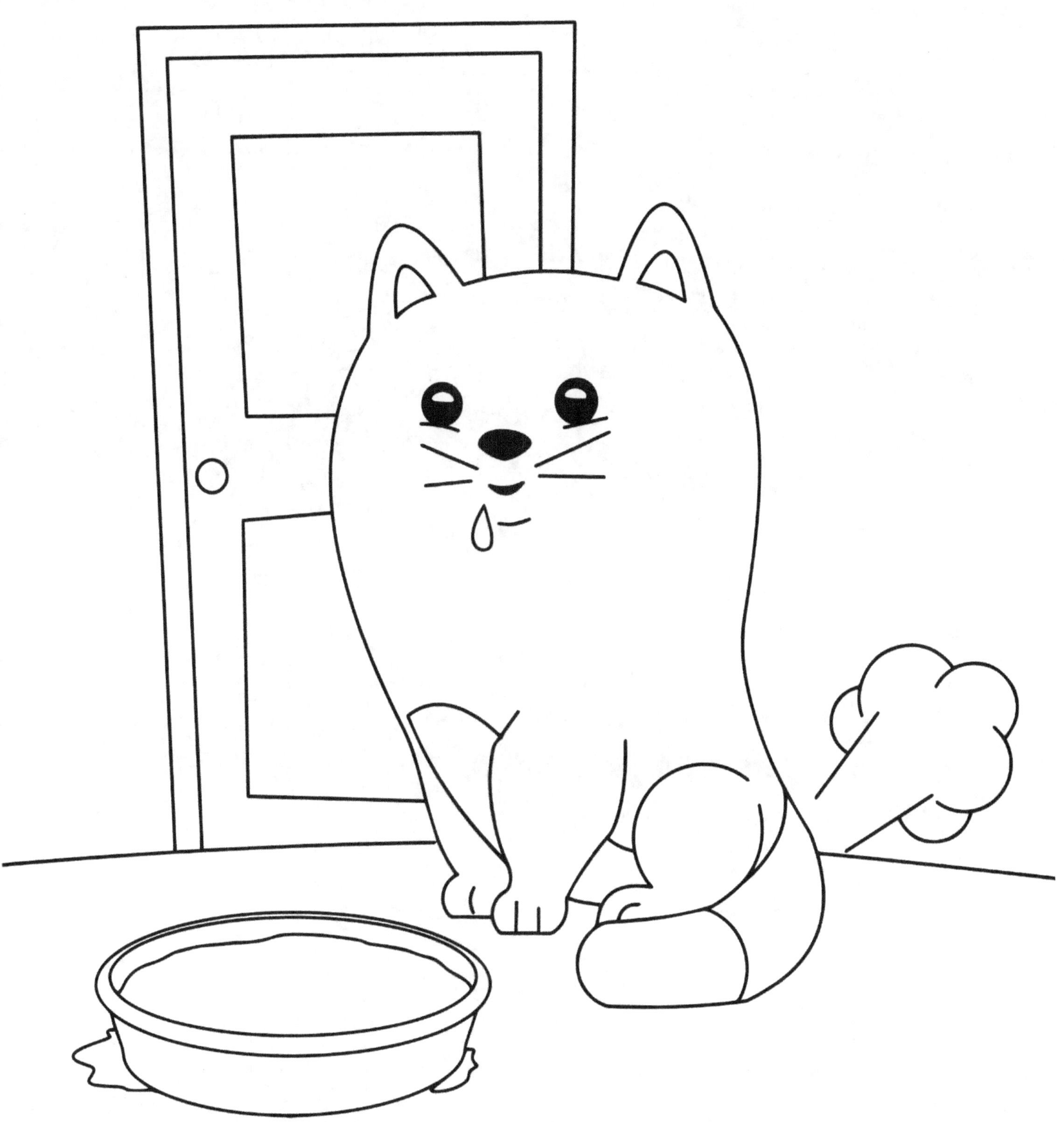

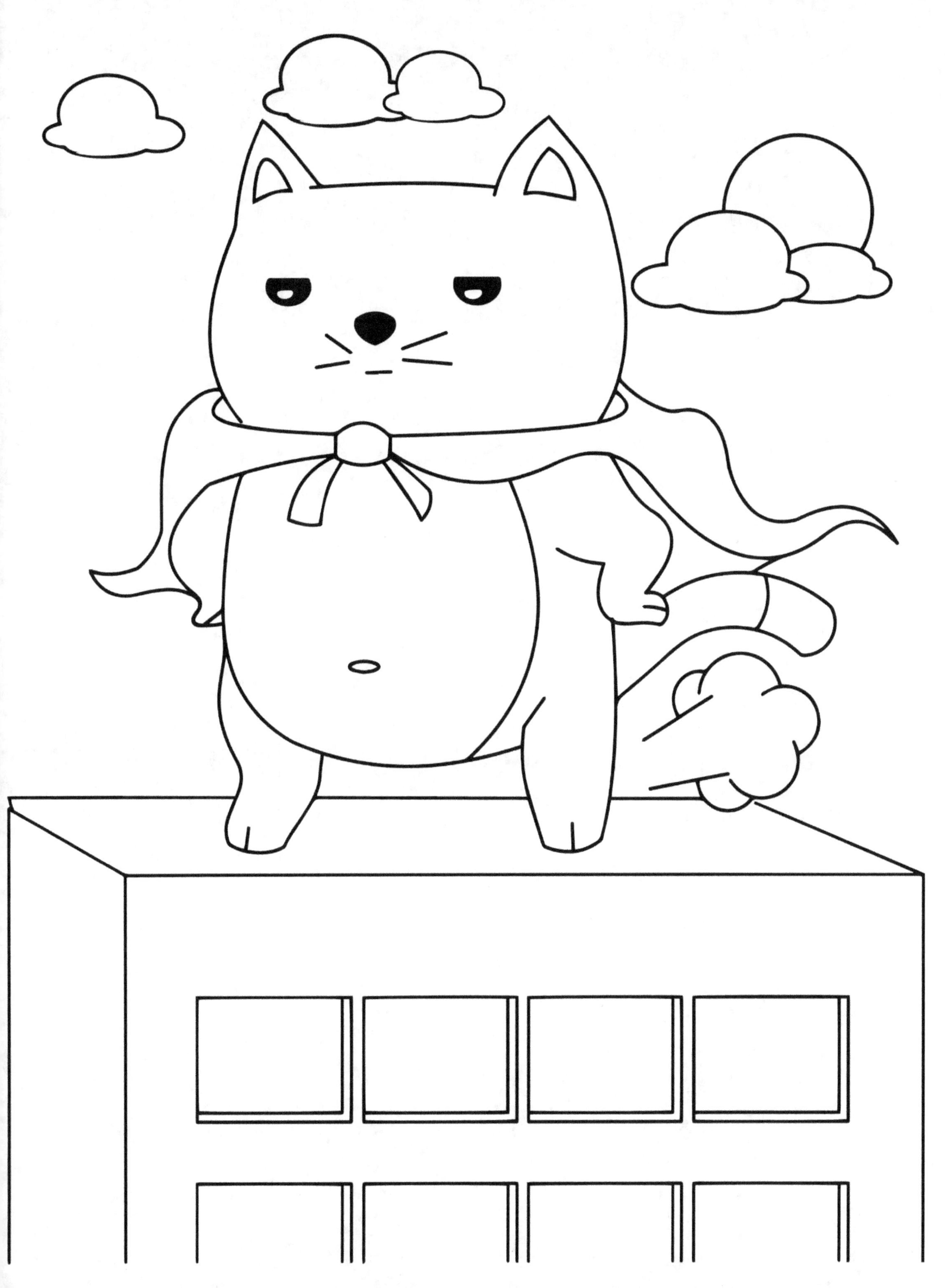

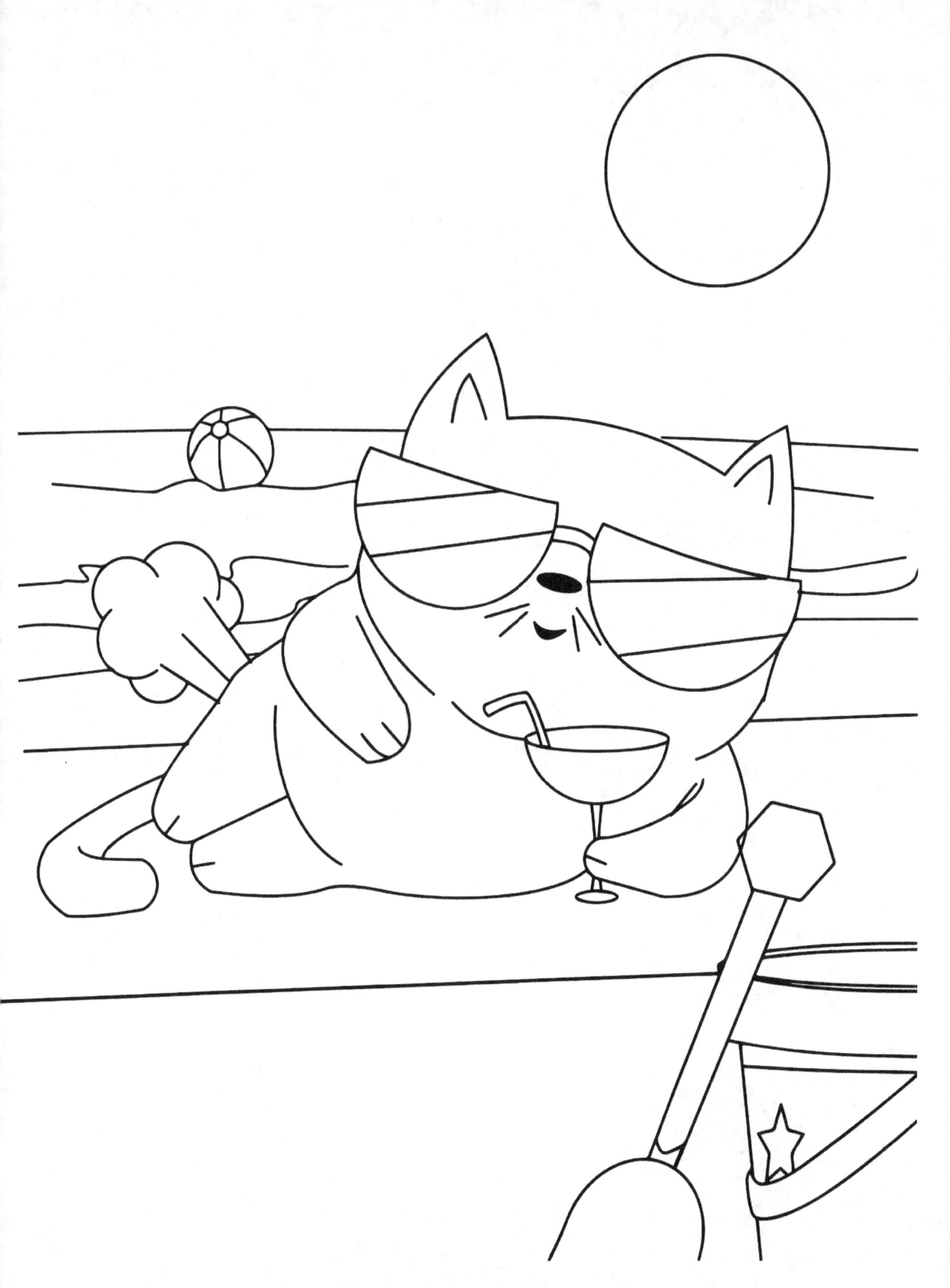

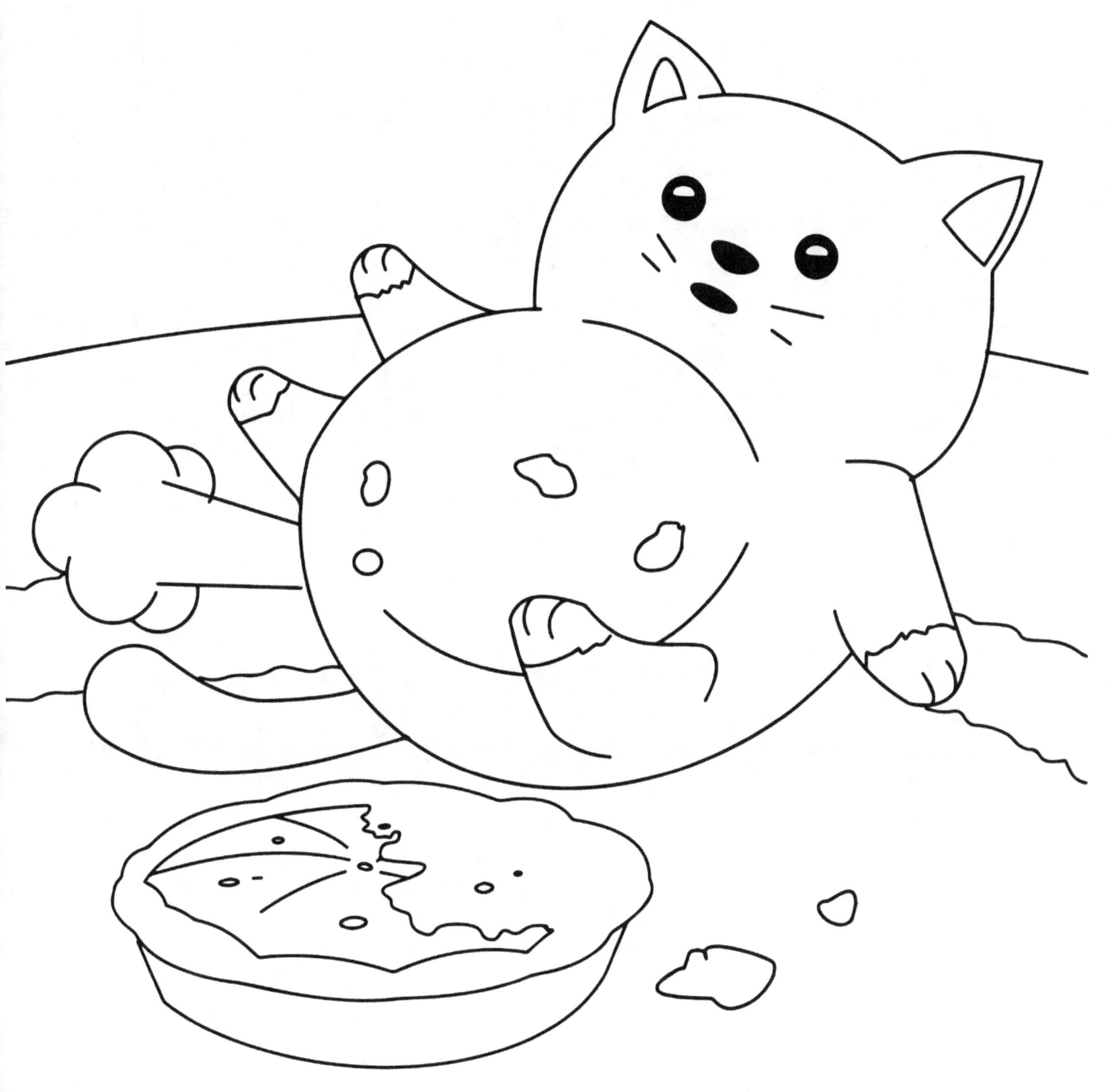

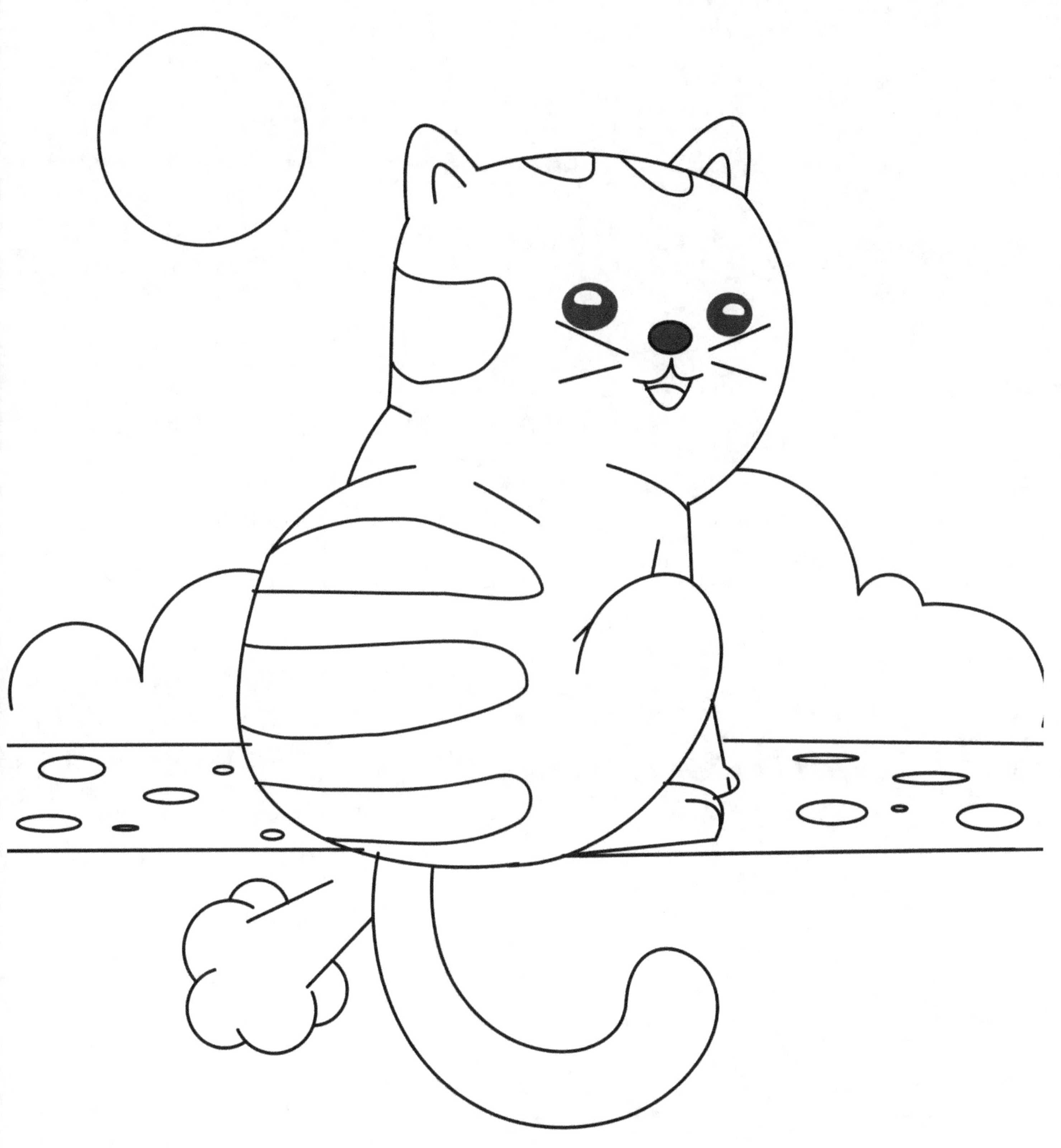

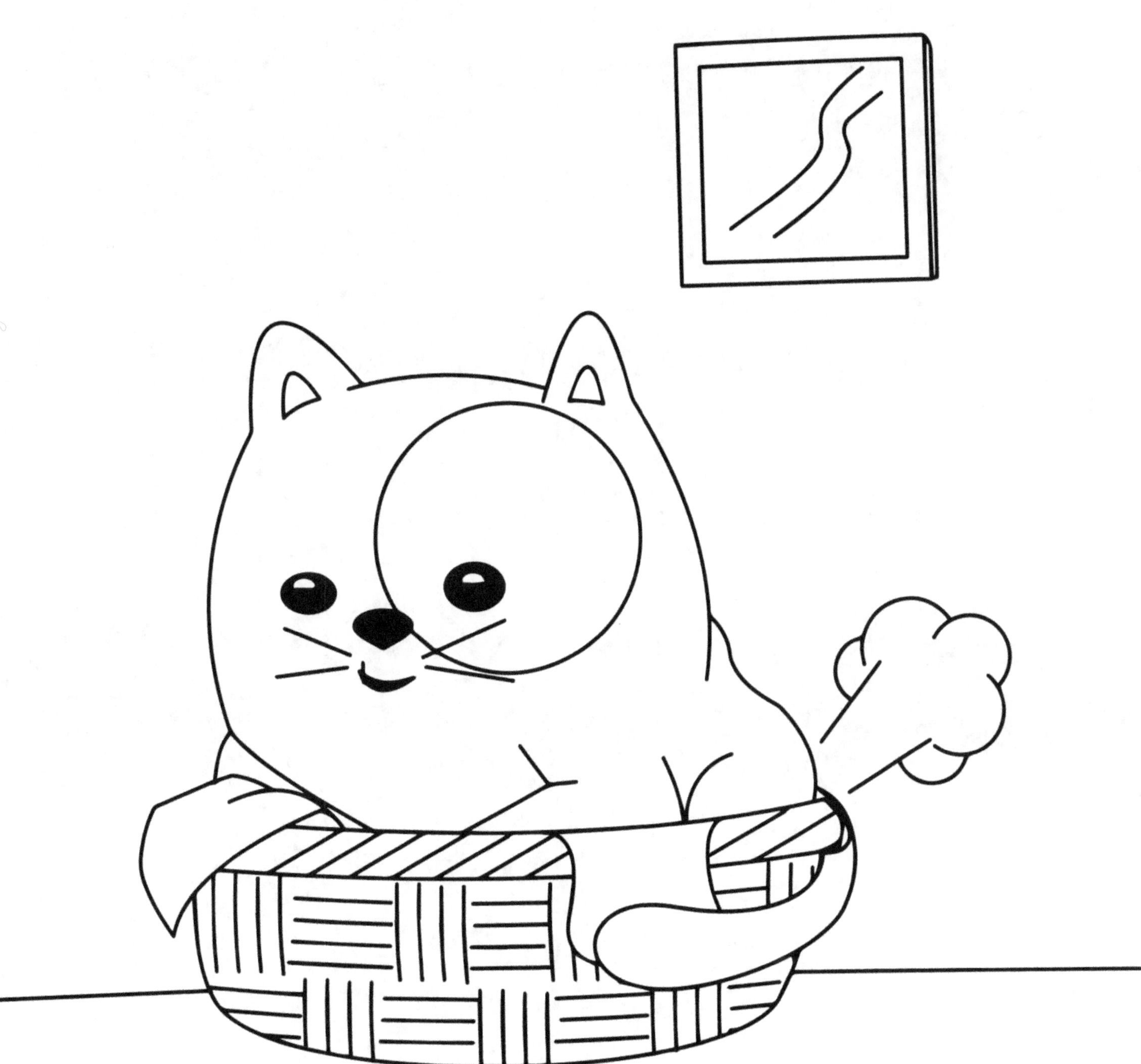

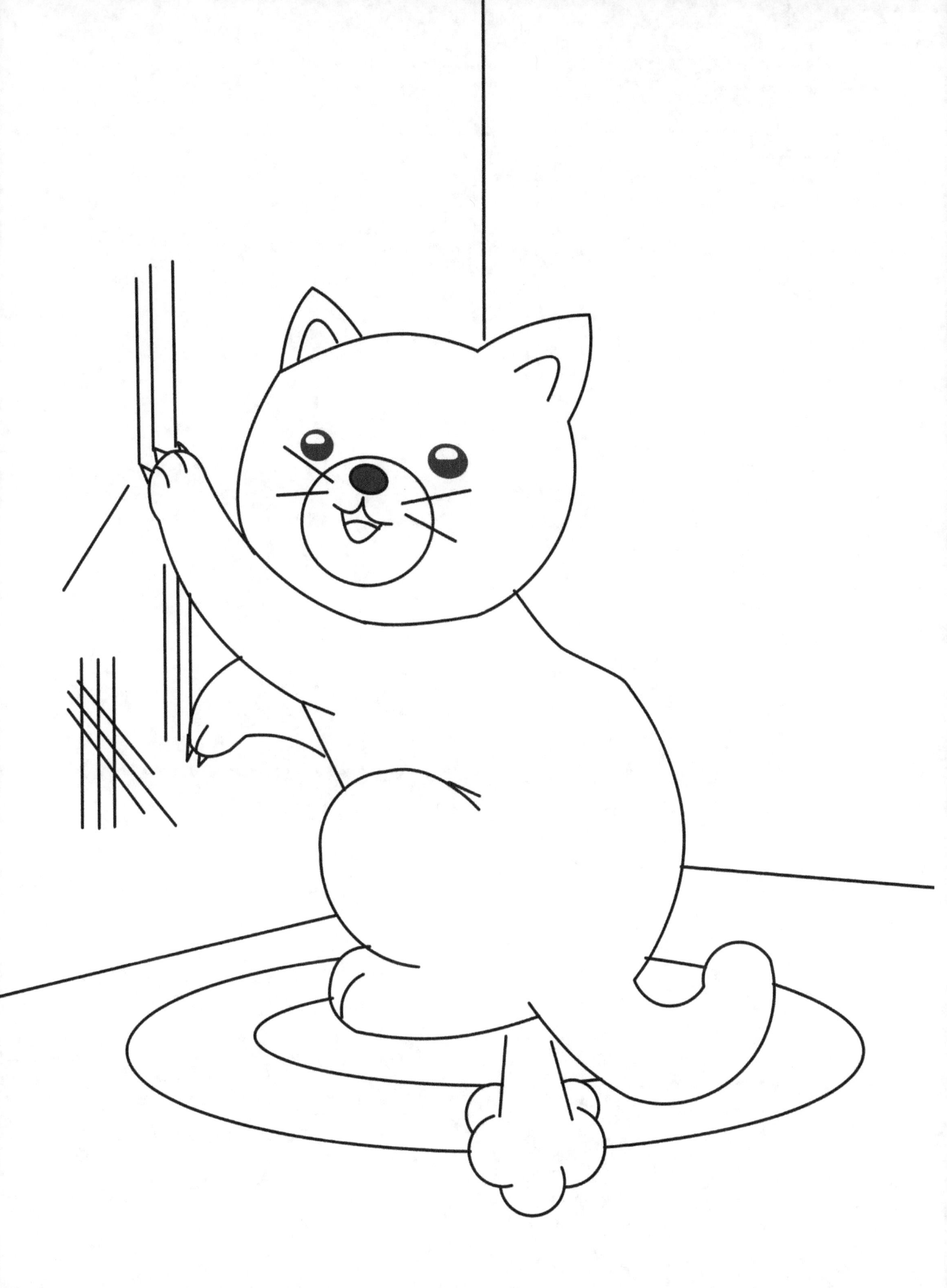

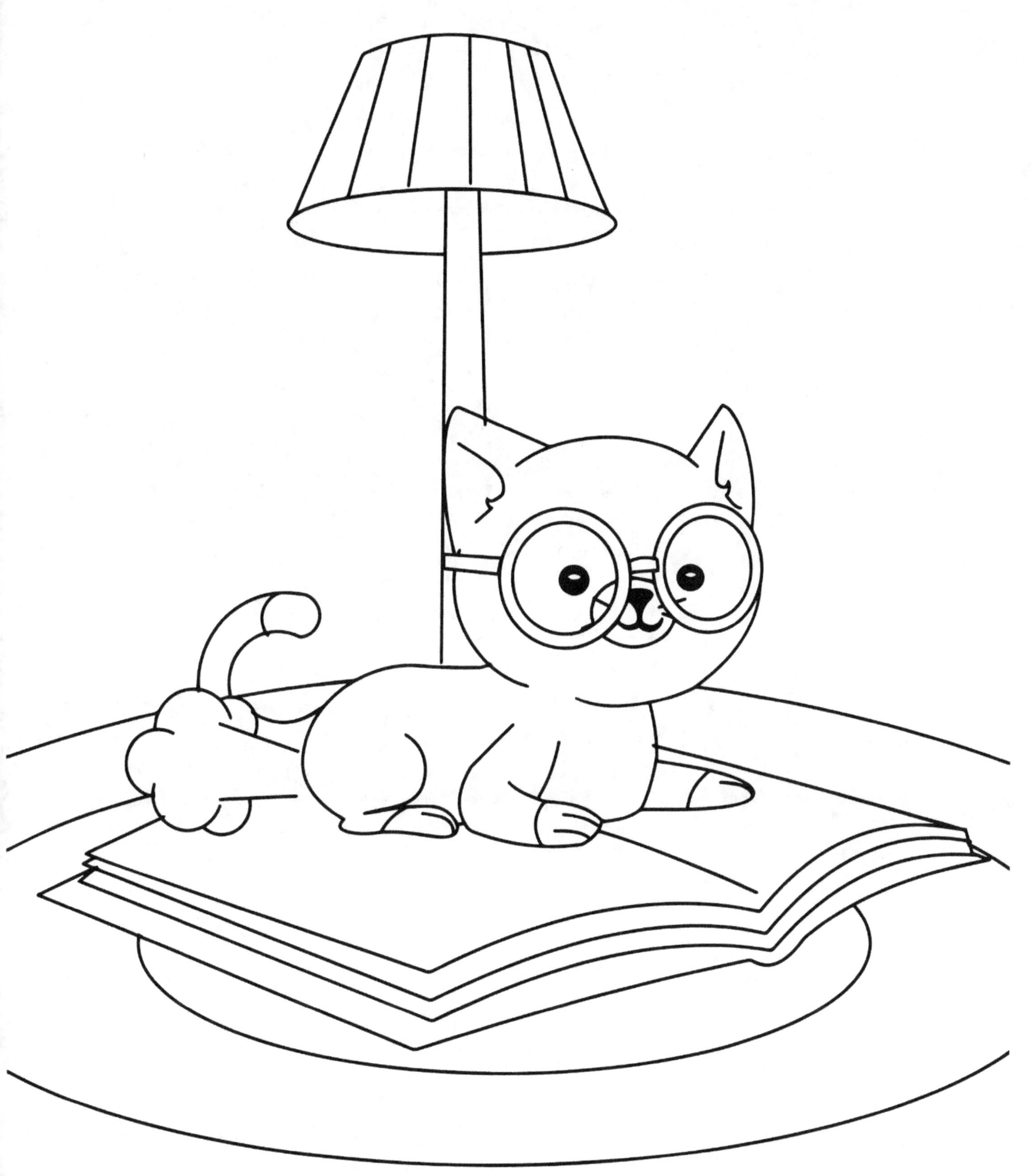

www.ingramcontent.com/pod-product-compliance
Lightning Source LLC
Chambersburg PA
CBHW081431250726
48654CB00013B/1910